Aliens

EXTRATERRESTRIAL
TALES OF TERROR

by Don Wulffson

Lowell House House
Juvenile
Los Angeles

CONTEMPORARY BOOKS
Chicago

ISBN: 1-56565-488-9

Library of Congress Catalog Card Number is 96-2988

Publisher: Jack Artenstein
General Manager, Juvenile Division: Elizabeth Amos
Director of Publishing Services: Rena Copperman
Editor in Chief of Fiction, Juvenile Division: Barbara Schoichet
Managing Editor, Juvenile Division: Lindsey Hay
Art Director: Lisa-Theresa Lenthall

Lowell House books can be purchased at special discounts when ordered in bulk for premiums and special sales. Contact Department JH at the following address:
Lowell House Juvenile
2029 Century Park East, Suite 3290
Los Angeles, CA 90067

Manufactured in the United States of America

10 9 8 7 6 5 4 3 2

Aliens

CONTENTS

For Maggie, my constant companion in our own alternate reality.

—*D.W.*

SCIENTIFIC EXAMINATION

Adventures made thirteen-year-old Kip excited, and today was the day. Finally the log raft he and his buddy Moog had worked on all week was ready to make its maiden voyage. They had finished building it yesterday afternoon, and today they were going to try it out on the Loki Swamp—a zillion miles of weird, junglelike vegetation and gross, slimy water, all full of disgusting animals, insects, and reptiles. The best place in the world for having an adventure!

Naturally, Kip didn't tell his mother and father what he was up to. Why tell them? It would only make them worry. Besides, they wouldn't have let him go.

They were so overprotective of him ever since there'd been stories of disappearances. Moog complained of the same thing. That's why the adventure they had planned for today was very important to keep a secret.

As he tramped down the dirt road toward the swamp on his way to meet Moog, Kip guessed that it probably was about a thousand degrees out. But the heat didn't bother him at all. He was too excited to think about anything as insignificant as the weather as he left the dirt road and made his way down through the woods that led to the swamp.

When Kip finally got down to the water's edge, he found Moog trying to launch the heavy, clumsy raft by himself. He was grunting and groaning and gallons of sweat were pouring off of him as he struggled with the awkward craft. "About time you got here!" Moog yelled, obviously annoyed.

"Sorry I'm late," Kip said. Then he got on the other end of the small raft, and together he and Moog finally managed to get it into the water. Made of about seven logs bound together by ropes, the small raft made a big splash, bobbed up and down, then glided off a few feet from shore.

Quickly, the two friends sloshed through the icky, green-tinted water after it. Then, after tossing rafting poles they'd made out of nimrod cane onto the deck, they crawled onboard themselves.

A minute later they were on their way, poling off into the deep, dark swamp, and seconds later Kip started talking away about this, that, and everything. Moog, however, being the silent type, hardly answered. Finally, he told Kip to be quiet, that his chattering was bothering him. Of course, "bothering him" was not how Moog put it. He used a little bit different language to describe how Kip's babbling was getting to him. But Kip got the message and shut his trap.

For a while the two continued on in silence, each digging his pole deep into the shallow, putrid water. In some places there was a thin, skinlike coating of yellow slime, and, unable to help himself, Kip joked, "Hey, Moog! Why don't you hop in and go for a swim?"

"Sure," Moog said, "right after you take a big drink of the stuff!"

Both smiling, they floated farther into the heart of the swamp, into areas they'd never even known existed. "It's like we're the only two individuals on the planet," Kip said, as the swamp ahead broadened into an inky-black lake.

"Yeah," Moog agreed. "And no one knows where we are."

As they continued on, the swamp narrowed again and overhead a cluster of towering trees created a vast, leafy canopy that almost completely blotted out the sun. "This is spooky," Kip said, looking up to see only little dots and specks of yellow light glinting through the greenery high above.

"And we're not alone in here," Moog cocked his head to listen. "I can feel it."

All around, in the creepy twilight world through which they were passing, an eerie orchestra of sounds was starting up. Unseen things slithered and rustled about in the vegetation, and a few batlike creatures flapped through the air, squawking and sending out ghostly, lonely-sounding calls.

Suddenly, Moog held up a hand. "Shh!" he whispered. Then he pointed with his pole. A big orange-and-white striped snake had coasted out from a pile of rotting underbrush and was wiggling almost straight at the raft. Moog knelt and leaned out over the side. In a flash, he grabbed hold of the creature and pulled its long, dripping body from the water.

"Cool!" Moog exclaimed, totally unafraid of the odd-looking snake. "I've never seen a reptile quite like this one. It's beautiful, in a way."

Kip recoiled in fear. He had to admit the snake was kind of pretty, but it was also very scary-looking, the way it coiled its long body around of Moog's arms.

Kip smiled and shook his head at his friend with admiration. "Boy, are you ever brave!"

"Not really," Moog said with a shrug. "I'm sure it's more afraid of us than we are of it." And with that he petted the snake's head a little just to show the creature he meant it no harm.

Kip looked into the creature's eyes. "It does look a little frightened," he admitted. But just then some of the fearful look went away, replaced by what Kip thought was a pleading look. "I think we should let the poor thing go. We must look like monsters to it."

Moog agreed, and carefully uncoiled the snake from around his arm. Then he let it glide off into the water, back toward the clump of decaying vegetation from which it had emerged.

The snake forgotten, Kip and Moog went back to poling their raft. Soon the gigantic trees became fewer and fewer, and the two buddies found themselves missing the shade the trees' cover had afforded them. For now the sun was at its full force, beating down on them, practically cooking them. In fact, it was so hot that the water seemed to actually be boiling, as little eddies of steam rose all around them and swirled around on the surface of the murky water.

"I'm tired," Kip moaned, dripping with sweat. "And look at this." He held his hand out to show Moog the blisters that had sprouted on his palms from the constant poling.

Sweat pouring from his own forehead, Moog nodded. "I'm pretty beat myself," he said. "Let's land this thing and take a rest on shore for a while."

They began to keep a lookout for an island or a good sandbar to land on, and soon found a large strip of earth that looked like a perfect place to disembark and begin their exploration on dry land.

Tired to the bone, they headed the raft toward the island and when they were close enough, they jumped out into knee-deep water and dragged the heavy raft onto shore.

For a while they just sat there, lazily talking. Then they got up and looked about the little island. But unfortunately, there wasn't much there—just some brambly bushes and a few clumps of spine reed growing out of the soggy soil. Bored with the place, they headed back to the raft … and that's when they heard it.

"Do you hear what I hear?" Kip asked, referring to an odd throbbing noise that seemed to be coming from overhead, from way overhead.

Moog nodded, and the two looked upward, but could see nothing. Not at first. Then suddenly he pointed at what appeared to be just a dark spot in the sky very far away. "What do you suppose it is?" he asked, wondering how something so small could make so much noise.

Kip was about to respond, when suddenly, with one scary whoosh, the thing zoomed down at them. And then it was there—a huge spaceship of some kind, hovering right above them, its engine quivering.

Terrified, Kip and Moog stared at the metallic gray craft, its glowing white dome pulsing, its rows of red lights blinking. And then a door in the bottom slid open with a hiss.

Kip backed away. "Run!" he yelled.

But Moog seemed rooted to the spot, paralyzed with fear. And in the next instant, a metal arm with a clawlike hand shot down. Moog screamed as the metal claw locked onto him, then retracted back up into the spaceship. The door closed, and Moog was gone.

Shrieking in horror for his friend and afraid he'd be captured next, Kip ran into the rank water. Frantic, he sloshed through the shallows, then dove under, plunging deep below the surface through inky blackness where he hoped he couldn't be seen. But how long could he stay under? One agonizing minute went by, then two. Finally, his lungs ready to burst, Kip shot to the surface. Gasping for breath, he looked around, then upward. The spaceship was nowhere in sight and there was no sign of Moog, either. Still, Kip could hear the same throbbing noise.

Ahead, there was a short stretch of open water. He swam toward it, sometimes above the surface, sometimes below. Then moments later he found himself amidst a thick strand of reeds growing up out of the water. He thrashed and crunched right through the reeds, and then he felt the bottom underfoot. His breath coming in heaving gulps, Kip crawled onto a muddy shore and collapsed on the ground. There was still no sign of the spacecraft, but the throbbing sound was still in the air.

Glancing over his shoulder, Kip rose to a half-crouch, then scrambled into a junglelike area. As he slogged along through ankle-deep mud, slipping and stumbling over tangled roots and fallen, rotting trees, Kip kept thinking of his dear friend. But there was nothing he could do for Moog. Now, all he could hope for was to save himself.

He tried to run—at least move as fast as he could—but the going was difficult along the narrow passageways clogged with vegetation. Suddenly, he froze. Directly ahead, on the ground in a large clearing, was the spaceship!

Terrified, he backtracked, then quietly hurried off in a different direction that took him up a gentle slope and into a forest of black-barked trees. Here, all was quiet. Even the pulsing sound of the ship was gone. He stopped for a moment, listening and looking all around the dark trees that surrounded him.

Then suddenly he almost jumped out of his skin. Was it his imagination, or had he just heard footsteps? Standing perfectly still, not moving a muscle, not even daring to breathe, Kip strained to listen, but there wasn't a sound, not a single sound until ... *crunch!*

They were standing right behind him!

Screaming in terror, Kip backed away, sickened at the sight of the aliens—huge creatures, with smooth, round transparent heads and gray skin that hung in ugly, loose folds.

He turned and ran ... right into the arms of another one.

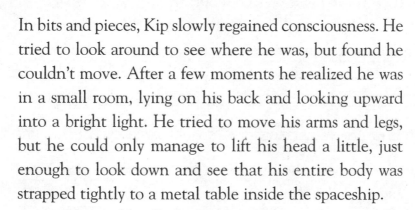

In bits and pieces, Kip slowly regained consciousness. He tried to look around to see where he was, but found he couldn't move. After a few moments he realized he was in a small room, lying on his back and looking upward into a bright light. He tried to move his arms and legs, but he could only manage to lift his head a little, just enough to look down and see that his entire body was strapped tightly to a metal table inside the spaceship.

He could tell that's where he was because the familiar vibrating of the ship's engine was all around him. It sounded softer, a bit different though—now that he was inside the thing.

Kip could also tell that they were moving because the cold metal table beneath him rocked and jiggled now and then. Yes, the spacecraft was bouncing on air currents, tilting one way and the other as it streaked along, taking him away—somewhere into space far, far from his home.

For a moment Kip struggled against his restraints. But the metal cuffs on his arms and legs held fast. Helpless, he lay back and let out an anguished cry.

Suddenly a door in the wall rolled open and an alien stepped into the room. Kip cringed in terror as it leaned over and looked at him, its eyes blinking inside its transparent head. Then it poked him with a rubber-looking hand, said something Kip couldn't understand, then turned and pressed a button on a wall.

Kip heard a door hiss open behind him, and immediately he felt himself moving—riding backwards as the alien pushed the shiny, wheeled table he lay on down a long corridor through the vessel. Looking from side to side as he was rolled along, Kip was sickened by what he saw.

There, lining the walls of the corridor, were cages filled with creatures from different planets. With hands, tentacles, and claws gripping the bars of their prisons, each creature watched as Kip rolled past, and each jabbered and cried out in its own language. They all seemed to be pleading with Kip to do something, to somehow set them free.

But what could he do? Kip wanted to tell them that he couldn't even help himself, let alone do anything for them.

The wheeled table turned a corner, and they entered another corridor. This one was even worse than the last. Far worse! Actually built into the walls were large, see-through containers, and in them were dead creatures—and *parts* of dead creatures—floating in some kind of clear, thick-looking liquid. Floating in one of the containers was an animal that was only a big round face with dozens of tentacles. In another was a bearlike animal, with a sweet, sad face, its eyes open and frozen in a death stare.

As the table rattled along, Kip saw dozens of specimens from other planets, from other worlds. It was unbearable seeing them—each looking so harmless, so innocent ... just like him.

Finally, Kip was wheeled past another metal table, and on it was ...

"Moog!" Kip shouted with joy. But his happiness soon turned to grief. It was just too horrible to be true. His friend, his buddy, was dead, lying on the metal table like a gutted fish.

"Nooo!" Kip screamed. And then he fell silent, sobbing quietly.

As he continued being pushed along, resolved to his own fate, Kip closed his eyes and thought of all the good times he and his friend had had together. He thought of Moog's family and his own, and realized that by now they were probably out searching for them, calling their names, looking for them in all the usual places they might be.

But they would probably never find them, not alive—certainly not Moog, anyway.

Behind Kip another door opened, and he was wheeled into a large room. It had a strong, sharp smell, and everywhere there was strange equipment and sharp-looking instruments.

Suddenly Kip heard footsteps—lots of them—coming from a room off the side. He turned his head as several more aliens entered. All of them were yammering about something, and then Kip saw them do something he just couldn't believe. They each reached up and took off their shiny heads—inside each of which was another head! If that wasn't gross enough, they then took off their outer bodies, peeling off gray folds of skin and actually hanging it from little hooks on the wall—right next to shelves where they had placed their horrible bulbous heads!

Kip's heart raced as fear coursed through every part of him. He knew they were going to do to him what they had done to Moog … or worse. To the aliens, he and Moog were just some kind of creature to be poked and probed and examined—for no other possible reason than to satisfy their sick, morbid curiosity.

Almost as if responding to his thoughts, five of the aliens came over to the table and stood over him. Kip went rigid with terror, and the eye in the middle of his forehead bulged out in fear as an alien placed a mask over both of his gaping mouths. Then a strong-smelling chemical began to fill the mask, and before Kip knew it, his quivering arms and legs—all sixteen of them—went limp as his world went black.

"Weird-looking beast, isn't it?" Dr. Jones commented as he bent over the alien with a scalpel.

Dr. Haley nodded. "But interesting," he said. "Unusual stomach area, and I'm quite intrigued by the single eye. It appears to be ocellic, similar, at least in its exterior morphology, to that of the genus Nematocera."

"Exactly what I was thinking," Dr. Barrera chimed in.

"If you don't mind, Frank," Dr. Feingold said to Dr. Haley, "I would like to get to work on the head first. That way I can make an RNA comparison with the encephalon of the other specimen that we brought in earlier."

"Sure, Susan. No problem," Dr. Haley replied, then he swung the overhead microphone of a disk-recorder closer to his face. He cleared his throat, then flipped on the recorder. "The date is July 8, 2156," he began, "and this is Dr. Frank Haley, Medical Director of the Apollo 42 U. S. Bio-space Collection mission. Doctors Jones, Barrera, and Feingold are in attendance as we prepare to examine one of two sub-sapiens captured this day on the unnamed planet coded 74019-BNQ on the extra-galactic map."

Dr. Haley stared down at the creature he was about to dissect and cleared his throat. "The specimen appears to be a male, about thirteen or fourteen Earth years old. We will begin by removing the head," he added, then pushed a foot pedal. In his rubber-gloved hand, an electric saw whirred to life.

ALIEN ANCESTORS

Arizona is home to the Red Rock Mountains, and Ronnie and his older sister Yvonne had been hiking there dozens of times. One of their favorite things to do was discover natural caves created by erosion, and already they had found and explored dozens of them.

But the one they found themselves standing in front of one summer afternoon during the hottest part of August was different than any cave they'd ever come across. Recent heavy rains had washed away the red claylike soil, exposing a deep opening in the side of the mountain that looked like it held all kinds of interesting rock formations.

Eleven-year-old Ronnie's eyes grew wide as he poked his head into the huge vertical fissure that cut deep into the mountain. "Boy, this is a *big* cave," he said, eagerly taking a flashlight out of his backpack. "Let's see where it goes."

Yvonne, three years older than her brother and therefore in charge, took off her glasses and cleaned them on her already filthy T-shirt. Putting her glasses back on and pausing a moment like a great explorer about to head off on a perilous adventure, she eased her slender frame through the narrow opening, flipped on her flashlight, and said simply, "Follow me."

Rolling his eyes at his sister's dramatics, Ronnie switched on his own flashlight and fell in behind her.

Once inside, the two instantly found themselves standing on a rocky ledge only a few feet wide. Before them was a yawning cavern, the floor of which was an obstacle course of huge, block-shaped boulders. They allowed themselves a moment to get used to the darkness and the stale humid air, then moved on.

"It sort of stinks in here but it's neat!" Ronnie said excitedly, his flashlight beam cutting into the darkness as he took the lead. "I don't think anybody's ever been in this cave before."

"You might be right," Yvonne agreed, following her brother as they weaved their way past the blocks of stone. "We may have discovered a brand-new cave."

At the far end of the cavern was a dark, winding tunnel that sloped gently downward. Rounding a bend, Ronnie and Yvonne were amazed to find themselves coming out of the tunnel into a vast chamber unlike anything they had ever seen before. It was immense, the rear wall even too far away to be picked up by the meager beams of their flashlights.

"Wow!" Yvonne gasped, her words echoing over and over. "This is beautiful!"

"Yeah, it's like a huge underground room!" Ronnie exclaimed.

The ceiling, a massive crystalline dome, looked like part of a huge cathedral. It was studded with long, toothy stalactites, tan and pink deposits of calcium carbonate, that hung downward like icicles. Below these were stalagmites, fatter, less delicate formations that were orange-hued and pushed up from the ground like inverted carrots.

"I haven't ever seen anything like this," Yvonne whispered reverently as she and her brother played their lights across the ceiling and walls of the underground chamber, picking out countless rock formations. Directly overhead there were bunches of slender tubes that looked like glass soda straws. And now and then, growing out of the walls, were red crystal flowers, some that actually had water dripping from the petals. Finally, down the center of the ceiling, almost dividing the cavern in two, was a great hanging curtain of stone, with folds like the garment of an ancient Greek goddess.

"This place is more like a museum than a cave," Yvonne said, her voice sounding hollow as it bounced off the cave walls. "Come on, let's keep going."

Ronnie was just about to follow her when his flashlight beam suddenly fell on something etched into the wall. "Hey, Yvonne, wait up," he called. "Take a look at this."

Yvonne directed her flashlight beam toward the wall where her brother's now shone. "It looks like a drawing of a person," she said.

"Look at the hands, though," Ronnie added. "It has only three fingers. And the face has only one eye."

"Creepy!" Yvonne exclaimed. "It looks like an alien or something!"

"Wow! Let's see what else is in here," Ronnie said eagerly. He headed up a corkscrewing passage with Yvonne right on his heels. It seemed to go on forever, winding around and around. Then, after ducking under a low archway of stone and rounding a sharp bend, they found themselves standing before a stairway of ancient, hand-hewn steps.

"Somebody used to live in here," Yvonne gasped. "Somebody had to have made this stairway."

"What if it wasn't some*body*, but some*thing*? Ronnie said, a nervous edge to this voice. "You know, like the drawings we just saw." He paused for a moment, looking around. "Maybe we should go back, Yvonne. I mean, maybe whoever or whatever lived here still does. Maybe they're up ahead just waiting to attack us!"

Yvonne's eyes lit up. "Yeah, and that would make this cave the find of the century. Listen to me Ronnie. We might have actually discovered an entire underground civilization!"

Ronnie frowned, his brow wrinkling. "But what if it's not a *friendly* civilization?"

Yvonne put an arm around her brother. "Don't start freaking on me, Ronnie. We may have stumbled onto something really big here. Now, are you with me or not?"

Not wanting to let down his sister, Ronnie reluctantly followed Yvonne up the strange staircase, their heavy hiking boots causing eerie echoes with every footfall. At the top of the stairs was a long, dark corridor. It was boxlike, a black rectangle that appeared to have been cut by hand through solid stone.

Yvonne took a deep breath. "Well, we've come this far," she said. "Let's go."

"Look, Yvonne. Maybe we've gone far enough," Ronnie said fearfully as he shone his light ahead into the tunnel. The dark seemed to swallow up the feeble beam. "Who knows what's at the end of this thing!"

"Only one way to find out," Yvonne said. She arched a brow. "But if you're too scared and want to wait here while I go ahead …"

"Go on," Ronnie growled. "I'm right behind you."

The air in the tunnel was hot and arid and seemingly without oxygen, and soon Ronnie and Yvonne were gasping for a good breath.

"Phew, I sure hope this tunnel ends soon," Yvonne panted, feeling as though the air was slowly being sucked from her lungs.

"I know, I can't breathe!" Ronnie gasped as he looked over his shoulder for the hundredth time, unable to shake the feeling that they were not alone. Meanwhile, to make things even more creepy, the echo effect in the dark tunnel was amplified, picking up Ronnie's last word and sending it back to him in threes, "Breathe! Breathe! Breathe!" as if mocking him.

Disoriented and frightened, the two hurried on, hoping that the tunnel would end before their lungs gave out. Both had decided not to speak anymore for fear of the menacing echo, and instead made their way in silence, using the rough stone walls to help guide them through the darkness.

Gradually, the tunnel began to brighten, and slowly the blackness softened to a dull gray. Then, as the ground beneath them made a sharp decline, they found themselves approaching a rectangle of light.

"I think the tunnel's ending!" Ronnie cried with relief. "Look up ahead!"

Sure enough, they soon emerged from the dark corridor onto a broad shelf of rock. Together they stared, blinking away the blackness, waiting for their eyes to adjust to the amazing sight that lay before them.

"I can't believe this place!" Yvonne gasped.

"Neither can I!" Ronnie exclaimed.

Stretching before them was yet another huge cavern, this one with a ceiling fissured and pocked with holes. Dim sunlight filtered down through the small openings, lighting up what appeared to be the remains of an underground city.

In silent awe, Yvonne and Ronnie made their way down an embankment and entered the eerie, dead-looking world. Scattered about, rendered white by age, were cone-shaped houses. Built of plastered mud and stone, their walls were crumbled and encrusted with time-hardened powder. Toward the back of the cavern there were other dwellings—dozens of them—carved into the limestone itself. The whole place looked like a massive fossil of a civilization older than time could possibly record.

"Who lived here?" Ronnie wondered out loud. "We've got to come back here with a camera."

Yvonne nodded. "You're right. No one will ever believe this!"

Together they continued to wander through the silent world, when suddenly Yvonne stopped dead in her tracks and sucked in her breath. Curled at her feet lay the remnants of a skeleton, its bony fingers clutching rocklike knees of hardened white powder.

"It—it wasn't human," Ronnie stammered, his eyes gigantic. "L-look at the hands!"

The skeleton was small, and its arms were as long as its entire body, about two-and-a-half feet in length. The hands were thin, spidery-looking, and had only three fingers and no nails. The skull had only a single eye socket.

"It's some kind of prehistoric creature," Yvonne said. "But I've never seen anything like it in any of my school books."

"I think it was just a child," Ronnie added. "Look at how small it is."

"I think you're probably right," Yvonne said. She looked at her watch. "Come on, it's getting late and I want to look around some more."

Fueled by the excitement of their discovery, Ronnie and Yvonne pored over the remains of the lost city and soon found the fossilized remains of several more of the creatures, all of them as small or smaller than the first. In the cone-shaped dwellings there were simple furnishings and artifacts of various kinds— stools, tables, pottery, and spoonlike objects. Like the inhabitants of this strange underground world, all of the artifacts had been turned to stone.

For nearly an hour, they wandered through dwelling after dwelling, finding more of the strange-looking skeletons and the tools they once used. Soon they had made their way to the rear of the cave, and before them was a massive, smooth wall, pinkish in color and carved with intricate, detailed pictures.

"It's like an ancient mural," Yvonne said, her eyes wide with fascination. "Let's try to figure out what it means."

"Look, these carvings show some of the creatures." Ronnie pointed to numerous pictures in which the one-eyed, three-fingered beings appeared. "Boy, they're creepy-looking," he added with a shudder.

"That's an understatement if I ever heard one," Yvonne said with a nervous chuckle as she walked back and forth, studying each of the etchings carefully. Finally she stopped and put her hands on her hips. "I think I know what these pictures are," she announced. "I think they're supposed to show the history of these people and of what became of them."

"Okay, professor," Ronnie said, stepping back and folding his arms. "You tell me because I can't figure any of this out."

Yvonne made her way to the first of the pictures. "In the beginning they lived above the ground." She pointed at the picture. "See the hills and trees over there in the background?"

Ronnie nodded. "Yeah, there's even a sun."

"Right," Yvonne said. "And here in the foreground are teepeelike houses with the three-fingered, one-eyed beings going about their daily routine."

She moved on to the next picture. "And this carving shows that they lived during the same time as the dinosaurs."

Ronnie stared in awe. "Yeah, I recognize them from my science book. One is a Plateosaurus and the other is a Stegosaurus. They're from the Paleozoic era. That's like six hundred million years ago!"

"*Before* people were on Earth," Yvonne added.

They moved on, studying picture after picture. One showed something shooting toward Earth, and in the next the one-eyed creatures were running in terror from capsules that filled the sky and were falling all around them. An especially large etching showed the capsules opening, and crawling out of them were hairy, brutal-looking beasts. Wielding weapons, these beasts were butchering and killing everything in sight— including the dinosaurs and the mysterious creatures with the single eye and three-fingered hands.

"I think I'm beginning to understand the story these pictures are telling," Ronnie said.

Yvonne sighed. "Me too, and it's pretty scary."

In the picture they were now standing before, the beasts from the capsules were cooking and eating what they had killed. Others wore the dead skins of the hunted creatures, while others had decorated their bodies with parts of the corpses.

"Gross!" Ronnie cried with a violent shudder. "Those monsters from outer space were so barbaric!"

"That's exactly what they were," Yvonne said gravely, making her way to the last few pictures. "And at the end, the survivors of their horrible attack moved underground and lived—right down here in these caves. This is where they died out and became extinct." She paused for a moment as if in respect for the dead.

Ronnie still had a lot of questions. "But who were these one-eyed, three-fingered creatures?"

"They were the original inhabitants of Earth," Yvonne replied, her voice hollow.

Ronnie scratched his head. "And they all got killed off by aliens?"

Yvonne nodded, a solemn expression on her face.

"Okay, so if the weird creatures were the original inhabitants of this planet," Ronnie pressed, "then who were the monsters that came in the space capsules?"

"Us," said Yvonne.

"*Us!*" Ronnie cried. "What do you mean?"

"I mean, *we're* the descendants of beasts that came from somewhere in outer space."

"Then that means—" But Ronnie was unable to finish his sentance. All he could do was stare at his sister in disbelief.

"It means that we finally know how we came to be on Earth and what we really are," Yvonne said, tears welling in her eyes.

"What are we, Yvonne?" Ronnie asked, his voice trembling.

Yvonne put a hand on her brother's shoulder. "We're the aliens," she replied. "*We're* the ones who invaded Earth."

THE DASTASIAN INVASION

lmost suspended in air, Daphne lies on a bed that can't be seen by the human eye, like a magician's assistant in a show, she seems to be just hanging there on nothing. Jamaal, his long hair in dreadlocks, leans against a wall that is also seemingly not there. As for me, well, I am standing at an invisible door, clutching bars I can feel but cannot see. The three of us are in an invisible prison cell, and have been for the last few months.

Two Dastasian guards pass by our cell.

"Food!" I yell at them. "We haven't eaten today!"

"Quiet, Earth boy!" one of them says. His voice is odd, and doesn't sound quite human. Though he and the other Dastasians have learned English in order to communicate with us, their accents are strange and very difficult to understand.

The other guard says something to the one who has just spoken to me. He speaks in the chirpish wail of his native language, then the two laugh, and continue on their way.

"Come back!" I beg. "We're hungry. We need food or else we'll die!"

Daphne looks up at me listlessly. "Save your breath, Roy," she says, running her dry tongue over her chapped and cracking lips. "They'll feed us when they feel like it."

"We are only kept alive as curiosities, anyway," Jamaal says. He picks a flea from his chest and crushes it between filthy fingers. "Sideshow freaks, that's all we are to them."

Daphne nods. "Freaks to be taken from place to place on this horrid planet of theirs to be examined, tested, and put on display." She smiles grimly. "I suppose we should be grateful, though. Even if it was only by accident, at least we didn't end up like all the others back on Earth."

"Grateful!" Jamaal snaps. "For what? To live like this, imprisoned probably until the day we die! To have survived to see the end of it all! To be the last of a species! Forgive me, but I am *not* at all appreciative!"

Daphne turns away from him as a muffled sob escapes her. Jamaal, his head hanging, goes to her, puts a hand on her shoulder, and apologizes for his outburst.

I gaze through the invisible walls of our prison. First I see other cells holding more prisoners from Earth. Looking beyond, I see the landscape of Dastasia, which looks little different from that of many desert lands of Earth. Dastasians—hundreds of them—are going about their daily lives as if we imprisoned Earthlings don't even exist. Many travel by in vehicles —though to my eye, since I cannot actually see the vehicles they ride in, it looks as if they are just floating by on nothing. Others are working away in buildings. They're on different floors and going about what appear to be ordinary tasks. But I cannot see the buildings that cover them—or any structures of any kind—and to me the Dastasians seem to be walking around on several layers of air.

"Relax, Roy," Daphne says to me. "They'll feed us again ... or they won't."

"Yeah," I mutter. I feel around until my hand touches the back of an invisible chair. I find the seat, then sit down dejectedly. For a moment I look at Daphne. She was so pretty and full of life. But now she's ragged and dirty, and without hope. Only fourteen —a year younger than Jamaal and I are—she looks like a withered old woman. Jamaal, though, is suffering the most. He coughs incessantly, and his skin is covered with rashes. He's always scratching, and there are patches of his flesh that are now raw and bloody.

It seems like only yesterday that everything was normal. I was on Earth, and for the most part, I was a typical teenager. My greatest cares were making the baseball team, getting good grades, and saving up for a car of my own someday. Like everyone else, I took it for granted that the future would be like the past and that life would just go on in pretty much the same way it always had.

But looking back, I can start to see when the downfall of Earth began. It was in the summer of 2013, when all of a sudden there was this rash of UFO— unidentified flying object—sightings all over the world. Most of the people who claimed to have had a sighting described it as a streaking flash of light, though several individuals were more specific about what they saw.

I remember one woman who said she saw an "invisible tube full of people" flying slowly through the air. That woman was from Iowa. Then there was a man from Russia, who claimed he saw people "descending right from the sky as though they were standing on an invisible platform." And then some kid from Ireland thought it was "raining people."

Like just about everybody else, I thought these sightings were interesting but of no real importance. I thought they were probably made by phonies wanting to be famous, or by some raving lunatics who actually thought they did see people pouring down from the sky. So what if a bunch of screwballs all over the world were seeing flying saucers and aliens? I told myself. It wasn't the first time, and it probably wouldn't be the last. In fact, I decided, the tabloids had probably all gotten together to scare the living daylights out of everyone.

Anyway, by the end of August, it was just old news. Fewer and fewer sightings were reported. Then there were none. Everyone pretty much forgot about the whole thing, and reporters went back to reporting on the latest foods that were dangerous to our health.

And then the bizarre workmen started showing up here and there. At first, no one made any connection between the sightings and these guys—that is, no one even suspected they were aliens. After all, they looked just like ordinary people. Oh sure, they acted weird. In fact, the stuff they did was totally crazy. But just because people are nuts doesn't mean they're from another planet, right? Little green men with antennas and ray-guns—now *that's* what you would expect extraterrestrials to look like. Not like these guys—they looked like a bunch of carpenters with a few loose screws, if you know what I mean.

Anyway, I made jokes about these goofballs like everybody else—that is, until a bunch of them arrived just outside of our town, Santa Isabella, New Mexico. Places like London, Tokyo, Cairo, Boston—all the big cities—that's mostly where these little groups of odd workmen had begun cropping up. Then, just about overnight, they seemed to be everywhere, including Cajon Canyon, about a mile outside of Santa Isabella.

As soon as we heard the news, a few of my friends and I piled into Kenny Gibson's beat-up electra car and headed off down Highway 77 to get a look at them. As it turned out, we were some of the first ones on the scene, but it wasn't long before a ton of other people showed up. It seemed like just about everybody in town wanted to check out what was going on.

"Boy, they're *weeeird!*" I remember my girlfriend Cassandra exclaiming as soon as we got close enough to see them.

"What the heck are they doing?" Ben Marks asked, looking at the rest of us as though we somehow had the answer.

"Well, obviously they're crazy," Amy Nova replied, as if she were some kind of an expert. "They must be, don't you think, Roy?" she asked me.

I just shrugged and kept watching them work, totally fascinated.

Other than what they were doing, they looked just like ordinary guys. There were five of them—all wearing coveralls like regular workmen—but these guys never said a word, not to us and not to each other. Still, it seemed clear that the tallest of the bunch was in charge. The others seemed to look to him now and then for directions, which he gave by simply nodding, winking, or making some other gesture.

One man carefully measured the distance between two points and marked it. Another came over and checked his work, squinting one eye to gauge the accuracy of the calculations. Apparently satisfied, he picked up something, adjusted it to his liking, then went to work.

None of this would have been weird except that there really was nothing there but the men—nothing that my friends and I could see, anyway. I mean, these guys had no building materials—no hammers, no nails, no tools of any kind—and yet they were clearly building something … out of thin air.

"They look like clowns," Kenny whispered.

A lady in front of us turned her head in our direction. "More like mimes," she said.

"I've seen mimes at parks," Amy said. "But they're usually entertaining people for money."

"So what are these guys doing it for?" Cassandra asked. "I mean, look at them. They're out here in the middle of nowhere."

"Maybe it's a publicity stunt for a new movie," I suggested, obviously reaching.

"Nah," Kenny said. "There's got to be more to it than that. I heard on the news that groups of these workmen are cropping up in places all over the world."

We went back to watching. Two of the workers, a look of strain on their faces, appeared to be at either end of a heavy beam, carrying it to a designated place. With exaggerated relief, they set this imaginary beam down on an imaginary worktable. Then, while they went back for another, the tall worker picked up an unseen tool. Holding it steady with his left hand, he turned a crank with his right hand in a practiced, unhurried circular motion, as though working with a hand drill. Finishing up, he blew away imaginary wood shavings then grabbed up a phantom object—a bolt, perhaps—between his thumb and index finger, then inserted it through the pretend hole he'd drilled. All the while, another worker had been waiting and watching. Seeing his companion finish inserting the invisible bolt, he stepped forward and began tightening it with an invisible wrench.

Cassandra chuckled. "These guys ought to be put in straight jackets and locked—"

She stopped short. The tall worker was looking right at her, as though realizing for the first time that any of us were even there. Seeming to understand what she had said, he appeared to be angry for a moment, then went back to work.

"I don't get it," Kenny whispered. "Why are they going through all the motions of making something that isn't there?"

"Maybe they're *not* going through the motions," Cassandra suggested.

"What do you mean?" I asked.

"Well, maybe they *are* building something," she replied. "Maybe it's just something we can't see."

After I got home, I immediately went to the television to check out the news. My parents were already sitting in front of it, their eyes glued to the screen. Practically every reporter, commentator, and talk show host was trying to figure out who these workmen were and what they were up to. Most of the commentary focused on whether or not there was any connection between the earlier UFO sightings and these strange guys. Many reporters were convinced the workmen were aliens who were making fools of us, assembling something right under our noses that would later destroy us. But all the government officials interviewed dismissed that notion, claiming that the workmen were under investigation, and if any foul play was detected, they would be stopped immediately.

As I watched program after program, I became convinced the workmen were definitely from another planet, and they were probably watching our television broadcasts and laughing their heads off at how stupid we Earthlings are.

The next morning my buddies and I went back out to Cajon Canyon. There were even more sightseers than there had been the day before, and now newspeople, the sheriff, and a bunch of deputies were there, too. The mood of the crowd was totally different from what it had been the first day. Rather than interested and amused, everybody was sort of tense and worried. And it wasn't long before they became downright hostile.

"I want to know what these jerks are up to!" one man in the crowd yelled.

"And who are they?" someone else demanded. "Are they aliens, like they're saying on TV, or what?"

More and more people started shouting, and as the crowd pressed closer to where the workers were, the sheriff grabbed a megaphone and ordered everyone back. For a while he was able to calm everyone, and all of us just went back to watching. But soon rumblings began to ripple through the crowd again, and I heard the sheriff calling in for more back-up.

The workers seemed to be doing something different today. A couple of them still gave the impression they were assembling something, but all the others were digging. Two looked as if they were using invisible shovels and pick-axes; dirt was being hacked at, scooped up, and piled to one side as a long, narrow trench appeared in the ground. Another worker seemed to be operating a bulldozer. He was sitting in the air, a few feet off the ground, and was working invisible levers and controls. There were rumbling, squealing noises, and as we watched, a depression appeared in the ground as a mountain of dirt was lifted in the air then carried away.

It was about this time that the sheriff headed over to talk to the workers.

"You aren't breaking any laws that I know of," the sheriff said as he approached the tallest one. "But I want to know exactly what—" Suddenly the man stopped dead in his tracks, and fell over backwards. It was as if he had walked into a brick wall, but of course, there was nothing there.

He shook his head. Then, still looking a bit dazed and confused, he yelled back to his deputies, "They've got some kind of force-field! Get on the horn and call the National Guard in here!" Immediately, the crowd surged forward, and like the sheriff and his deputies, everybody began running their hands over an unseen barrier of some kind. My friends and I felt the thing, too. It was smooth, like clear plastic, but it had sort of an electrical feel to it that made my fingers tingle.

Within the hour a few units of the National Guard arrived on the scene. They tried nearly everything possible to get through the invisible barrier. They rammed it with trucks. They used a wrecking ball type device. They even tried explosives. Nothing worked.

Meanwhile, the workers just went about their business inside the invisible wall, acting as though nothing was happening.

Late that afternoon regular army troops showed up in force. Rockets, lasers, and napalm had no effect on the barrier. Even tanks slammed into it and were stopped dead in their tracks.

At this point, everyone was getting *really* scared, me included. The crowd broke up and people raced for their homes and locked themselves in.

During the next few days I only went out to Cajon Canyon a couple of times. Mostly I stayed home, transfixed by what I was seeing on the television. What had happened outside our town was happening all over the world. The workmen, shielded behind invisible force-fields, continued putting together whatever it was they were building. Finally, on the eighth day after their arrival, it seemed their job was done. The only thing they were doing was putting away their invisible tools and cleaning up.

Later on that same day, reports of even more unbelievable things started coming in on just about every channel, and live from around the world. But we didn't need television sets to see it. All we had to do was look outside. All our neighbors were out on their lawns and in the street, staring up at the sky with expressions of awe on their faces.

"It's impossible!" my dad exclaimed.

"It's like the UFO reports back in August," said our next-door neighbor, Mrs. Greenberg, her voice quaking. "It's like the sighting in Russia!"

I wouldn't have believed it if I hadn't seen it with my own eyes. There, raining down from the heavens, were "tubes" of people—hundreds of them. As I stared in utter amazement, I realized that "tubes" wasn't quite the right word. It was more like these people—rather, these aliens—were descending upon us from gigantic invisible escalators!

"We're being invaded," my mom said, her voice so soft it was as though she were divulging some kind of secret. "Those workers were like the vanguard, sent ahead to make way for the others."

"But what were they building?" I asked.

To that question, my mother just shrugged. "I'm afraid we might find out sooner than we want to."

It was at that moment that the humming—the music—began. Never before had I heard anything so beautiful. But the music wasn't just something I heard, I could *feel* it inside me. It went straight to the core of my being. Right to my soul, and I could see it was doing the same thing to everybody. It was enrapturing us, calling us … but to where?

Though it was clearly all most of us could think about, no one spoke about the music. Instead, without a word of discussion or a moment's second thought, we all started walking toward it, not caring where we were going, not knowing when we would get there, not even asking any questions. Smiling blissfully, everybody just kept walking.

Soon, the streets were filled with people—kids and adults, men and women, clerks and salespeople, lawyers, doctors, and teachers. Even the cops and military people dropped their weapons and began walking right along with us toward the source of the music.

Cajon Canyon is where we all ended up. Thousands of the Dastasians were there, and more were descending every moment, landing on the Earth like they already owned it. Of course, at the time, we didn't know what these aliens were called, and subdued by the music that filled our heads, we didn't seem to care.

With the force-field now apparently gone, the enthralling music led everyone in town straight toward the invisible thing the workers had built. Then all at once a whirring sound could be heard mixed in with the music. In retrospect, it should have terrified me, especially in light of what was happening to the people in front of me. But at the time, it didn't seem the least bit threatening or unusual to me that the line of people was slowly disappearing.

One by one, people were dropping out of sight. Cassandra and Kenny were a little ways ahead of me, and they looked happy and content as they vanished before my eyes. My next-door neighbors, the butcher, and my math teacher all went next—*poof!* They were gone. But I didn't care. I was ready—no I *wanted* to walk right after them into nothingness. But it wasn't to be.

At the last minute, I was pulled out of line. Angry, no infuriated—for that's how much I *needed* to go to that music—I had to be restrained by several Dastasians. I saw no reason why I should be denied the pleasure of total envelopment by that incredible music, that music that I desired more than anything in my whole life.

The flight to Dastasia—in a craft I could not see—felt like I was being hurled through space. It lasted no more than a few minutes, and it wasn't until I was thrown into the prison I now sit in that I met all the others who had been selected by the Dastasians to be studied, interrogated, and put on display.

Altogether, there are about a hundred of us in some twenty invisible cells. We come from different places on Earth and represent different age groups and different walks of life. My cellmates are Daphne from England and Jamaal from South Africa. My guess is that the three of us are supposed to be the typical teenager specimens.

In the cell next to ours there are two Asian kids and their mother and father. In the cell across the way is a group of scientists. And around a corner are military personnel, mostly high-ranking officers, both male and female of various ages.

Most of our guards are harsh and treat us like trash. A few, though, treat us decently, especially an elderly Dastasian named Hodur. He seems intelligent, and speaks English and several other of the languages of Earth. Though it is generally forbidden for guards to converse with prisoners, Hodur sometimes talks to me when the other guards aren't around.

Ever since I arrived here, I've been begging him to tell me what they're going to do with us. But, he just shakes his head and says he doesn't know.

"Well, what were they doing on Earth with everyone else?" I asked him one day.

"It is simple," Hodur replied. "Dasatia was over-populated. For more than forty Earth years we have been conducting reconnaissance flights throughout the galaxies. Finally it was decided that your planet was most like our own, and therefore, best suited to our needs. Plans for invasion and extermination of your species were drawn up."

"Why are Dastasian structures invisible?" I asked.

"They are only invisible to Earthlings, not to us," Hodur explained. "Your powers of perception are very limited and underdeveloped. We used this to our advantage, as you no doubt now realize, in formulating our plans for conquest."

I was burning to ask one more question, my last and most important, but Hodur fell silent and walked away at the approach of several guards. Not until this morning was I again able to talk to him and ask the question which had tormented me for so long.

"What was the invisible thing the workers were building?" I demanded. "Please, what difference does it make now that I am on your planet? Who could I tell?"

Hodur thought about this for a moment, then he replied. "It was a thing to get rid of Earthlings in the quickest and easiest way possible in order to make room for the Dastasian population."

"Yes, that much I know," I said impatiently. "But what *was* it?"

"Our word for the device is different from your own," he replied. "I can think of only one Earth word that has about the same meaning."

"And what's that?" I asked, remembering how I heard the whirring noise just before the people in front of me dropped from sight one by one.

Hodur looked extremely uncomfortable. "You must understand," he said, "that Dastasians have a very low opinion of Earthlings. For us they are little more than waste that had to be eliminated."

"Yes, I realize that!" I said, growing frustrated. "So tell me, what were you building all over my planet?"

"I believe," Hodur replied slowly, "that you call them garbage disposals."

THE KILLER OF FAYETVILLE

All sorts of questions arose: Why did the woman in the fancy dress end up dead, crumpled up near the bench at the bus stop? Why did our next-door neighbor, Mr. Benson, have to die undergoing an operation he didn't need? Why did more than two hundred people die when their plane crashed into a mountain that wasn't supposed to be there? Why? And why did so many other strange, sick things happen here in Fayetville? Maybe we'll never know.

It started on Tuesday, April 14, 2006—at about 2:09 P.M. I was at school—Adams Middle School—in my sixth period computer class. We were all at our lab stations and had turned on our computers. Our teacher, Ms. Nantes-Smith, was talking about how to create document templates.

"Does anyone have any experience in creating templates?" she asked the class.

Right away, nerdy Bobby Boaz, in the station next to mine, raised his hand and started waggling his fingers. "Ooooh ooooh, I do!" he cried.

"'Oooh oooh oooh,'" I mimicked with a laugh. "What are you, Bobby? Some kind of monkey?"

"Doug Whalen!" Ms. Nantes-Smith said, pointing at me. "Would you *please* stop disrupting the class!" Then she turned to El Geeko and smiled. "Please, go on, Bobby," she said, "Tell the class what you know about making a template. I promise—there will *not* be any more interruptions."

Boaz gave me a smug look. Then, acting like he was the teacher and we were his students, he started lecturing us on templates, even though it was obvious right off he didn't know what he was talking about. Meanwhile, Shondra Lake, on the other side of me, was giggling and watching as I unscrewed the plug connecting El Geeko's computer to the tabletop outlet. I had gotten the first screw out when out of the corner of my eye I saw my own computer monitor change. It had been blank, just a plain blue, but suddenly words appeared. They said: THE GAME BEGINS.

At first I thought it was only on my screen. But then Shondra grunted real loud, "Huh?"

And then the guy behind me, Oscar Freeman, tapped me on the shoulder and asked, "Hey, Doug, how'd that get on our monitors?"

In fact, everybody was checking out each other's screens, and we were all freaking out because **THE GAME BEGINS** had instantly appeared on each and every one of them.

"All right everyone, who's sending this message?" Ms. Nantes-Smith asked the class accusingly. "I want whoever is doing this to stop this instant."

But everybody just looked blankly at her.

A minute later Mr. Trent rushed into the room from the advanced computer lab next door. The same thing had suddenly appeared on all the monitors in his classroom, and he couldn't make any sense out of it either. And nothing he or Ms. Nantes-Smith did— including unplugging all of our computers—had any effect. The same three words still remained on all the monitors: **THE GAME BEGINS**.

We were just sitting there not knowing what to do when the principal burst in. She was really upset, and told us that the same weird message had appeared on every computer in the school. She seemed to think that one of us was responsible and looked each of us in the eye trying to get us to confess.

Then all of a sudden, the dismissal bell rang with forty minutes left in the school day. It didn't just ring for a couple of seconds, but kept going on and on with one long, steady ring.

Of course, all of us kids took immediate advantage of the situation and began piling out of the classrooms as fast as we could. And of course, the teachers all went nuts, yelling for us to come back. And did we? Not on your life! Yes indeed, those computers had been absolutely right. The game had definitely begun.

In front of school, I hooked up with Dori Hill, who is sort of my girlfriend and best buddy. She lives across the street, so we usually walk home together. We were almost two blocks from school when the bell finally stopped ringing.

"I wonder what caused all that weirdness?" Dori was saying as we went into a convenience store to get a couple of Sludgecicles. That's when we saw the cashier and a bunch of girls behind the counter staring at the cash register.

Apparently, the cashier had just rung up a pack of bubblegum and three candy bars, and the total on the register was $9,598.73! They were all confused and laughing. "It just went berserk all of a sudden," the cashier said, scratching his head.

"Hey, look at that," Dori said to me. "Another machine's gone crazy."

We left the store without our Sludgecicles, since the cashier decided he'd better close until the cash register was fixed. As we walked along, talking about what was going on, I stepped off the curb at Grover and Fayet, in the busiest part of town.

"Watch out!" Dori yelled, yanking me back.

"Huh?" I said, startled. The light at the crosswalk said WALK, but cars and pedestrians were fast approaching from every direction, and the traffic lights on every corner were green.

"Hey, what's going on?" I asked, twirling around in wonder.

All of a sudden the intersection had turned into a blur of colors slamming into each other, and the air was filled with the sound of squealing tires, banging metal, and shattering glass. I closed my eyes and sucked in my breath at the sound of all the screams that came next as several cars went up onto sidewalks and rammed into pedestrians.

"Wh-what's happening?" Dori sobbed.

I couldn't answer. I could only stand there with my knees shaking and the blood draining from my face, wondering if what I was seeing was more of "the game." If it was, it wasn't a game at all—it was nothing but a bloody horror show.

Suddenly a green van flipped across the street and skidded on its side in a fan of sparks toward Dori and me. We jumped out of the way just as it smashed through a plate glass store window. A man stumbled out of the wreckage with blood streaming down his face and Dori and I helped him over to a bench.

"I—I don't understand," he kept saying. "I—I don't understand."

Dori took the man's handkerchief out of his pocket and pressed it to the cut on his head, meanwhile, my attention was being pulled in another direction. My eyes were riveted on something else a few feet away. It was the body of a woman, her eyes fixed in a death stare. She had a fancy dress on, but no shoes.

My parents weren't home when I finally got there. Worried sick about them, I went with Dori over to her house. Her mom was staring at the TV, watching the news, a numb, sickly expression on her face.

"It seems to be happening all over town," she said. "Anything to do with electronics and computers has gone haywire. Streetlights are going off and on. False alarms keep coming in to the police and fire stations, while real emergency calls can't get through. People are stuck in elevators that just keep going up and down without stopping." She shook her head in dismay. "But the worst nightmare is at the airport. The air traffic controllers are getting false radar readings, and pilots are reporting weird messages from their on-board computers. One plane, descending through the cloud cover, slammed straight into a mountain because the pilot thought he was right on course to land."

Dori and I sat next to her mother on the couch. On the TV, rescue teams were slowly picking through wreckage. "So far, only two survivors have been found," a reporter said. "And the search for more continues."

"Is it happening in other towns, too?" Dori asked, "or just here in—"

"Only in Fayetville, according to the news," her mother interrupted, her eyes glued to the TV. "And they think someone right here in town is responsible. The police are searching for that person—or group of people, but so far they've come up empty."

"Why would anyone want to do this?" I asked.

Dori's mother shrugged. "There's no logic to a killer's mentality."

"Maybe someone's got a grudge against the whole town," Dori suggested.

Just then the phone rang and Dori's mom dragged herself off the couch and picked up the receiver.

"Hello? Who is this?" she asked, her voice tentative. "Hello? Hello?" Frowning, she hung up and started to walk away. But seconds later, the phone rang again. She snatched up the receiver, this time nearly shouting, "Hello!" But as she held the receiver to her ear, it kept ringing ... and it went right on ringing even after she'd already hung up.

Suddenly Dori looked at her mother and then at me. "That's strange," she muttered.

Then I heard it, and from the look on Dori's mother's face, so had she. In a daze, we all went out onto the front lawn. Other people were coming out of their houses, too. For in every house, office, restaurant, or phone booth, telephones were ringing. The sound grew louder until the air literally vibrated and our heads nearly burst, as every phone in Fayetville rang at once.

A few minutes later the ringing abruptly stopped. I saw my parents pulling into our driveway, and I ran across the street. One side of the car was scrunched in. I could see they'd been in an accident, but so many horrible things were going on at that moment, they didn't even bother to explain what had happened to the car.

We all went inside and were surprised to find Mrs. Benson, the elderly lady who lives next door, sitting in our living room. "I—I'm sorry," she stammered, dabbing at her teary eyes with a crumpled tissue. "I didn't know where else to go. The door was open, so I just—" She burst out sobbing hysterically.

Immediately my mother rushed over to the poor woman and sat down next to her. "It's all right, Mrs. Benson," she said sympathetically. "We're all concerned with what's going on." Then, little by little, she was able to get Mrs. Benson to tell her what had happened.

"My husband checked into the hospital this morning. He was going to have a minor operation on his foot," the elderly woman began. "But the hospital's computer checked him in under a different name ... and scheduled him for a heart transplant!" She burst into tears again. "He—he died on the operating table, and the man who was *supposed* to receive the new heart passed away a few hours later!"

"What kind of monster is doing this to us?" my mother gasped.

"Well, whoever's behind this," my father said grimly, "he or she has hit us where we're weakest. Civilization is at the mercy of electronics."

In horror, I realized that my dad was right. Someone smart enough—and cruel enough—could put an end to Fayetville—not to mention the whole world by simply flipping a switch.

"Do you think they know it's you?" ten-year-old Orson asked his sister Lela. He was in Lela's room, looking over her shoulder as she activated her multi-tiered, supersonic nuclear computer. "Is there any way they could figure it out?"

"I doubt it," twelve-year-old Lela replied with a giggle. "They're too stupid." She grinned maniacally and punched in another code. "Watch this."

Orson's eyes lit up as he watched the monitor. People were falling all over themselves trying to get to automatic tellers, all of which were shooting money out like crazy. "You'd better stop, Lela," he cried, laughing so hard tears were oozing out of his eyes. "They're going to kill each other!"

Suddenly, from down the hall they heard their mom calling them to dinner.

"Coming!" Lela yelled. Then she turned to her brother. "Darn, I was just getting warmed up!"

"You know what would be fun?" Orson grinned. "We could activate your computer game on an entirely different town tomorrow."

"I was thinking about doing it all over the Earth!" Lela exclaimed. "All I would have to do is a little reprogramming. The computer systems on Earth are primitive compared to those here on Venus. It's child's play to access and manipulate them."

Orson laughed. "Child's play!" he exclaimed. "Boy, are you ever right!"

"Lela! Orson!" their mother called, this time a little more insistently. "Come eat your dinner!"

"We'd better get going," Orson said. Extending his single jelly-leg from his shell, he liqui-glided across the marblesque floor. "Come on, Lela," he said through the mouth in the back of his head as he glided out the door. "I'll race you!"

Lela paused, her brain pulsating inside her transparent skull as she thought about what she would do to Earth in the morning. Then she reluctantly turned off her computer. "Last one there is a rotten slug!" she yelled. Then, following in Orson's gooey slime-trail, she glided out after her brother, her shell iridescent in the hot light of the second planet from the sun.

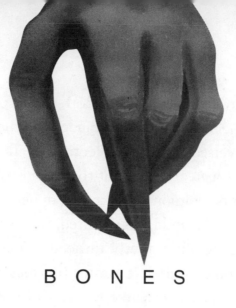

B O N E S

A small log cabin was home to Bud and Tami McNeil. Their life was a little different from that of most teenagers. Instead of living in a big city, or even in a little town, they lived with their mom and dad in the remote reaches of the White Mountains. They had no neighbors within a five-mile radius, and they had no television, no telephone, no electricity, and no running water. The most modern thing they owned was an old station wagon, and that mostly just sat moldering and rusting away in the high grass around the cabin.

Unlike most kids their age, Bud and Tami had never set foot in a schoolroom. But that didn't mean they weren't well-educated. Both their parents had been teachers, and they had made sure their children were well versed in every subject. True, Tami and Bud didn't know a great deal about the outside world, but in their parents' opinion they knew enough. They knew that the outside world was polluted, corrupt, crime-ridden, and generally a pretty unhealthy place for both the body and the mind. It was for this reason that their parents had decided to live the rest of their lives "in harmony with nature," as they put it, and to raise their children with a strong sense of the *natural*, not the technological, world.

Not much ever happened in the McNeil's rustic, peaceful hideaway. But one night there had been a loud crashing noise that had awakened the entire family. Tami and Bud's parents had immediately dismissed the noise as a sonic boom, possibly from another space shuttle breaking the sound barrier. But Tami and Bud hadn't been convinced by this explanation.

And so, the next morning, as soon as all their studies and chores were done, the two teenagers headed off into the forest, wondering if they might be able to find some other reason for the sound that had disturbed their sleep.

For hours they searched through the familiar woods, hiking farther than they'd ever gone before. But all their efforts turned up nothing.

"We're on nothing but a wild goose chase," Bud finally concluded, his face shiny with perspiration as they tramped along.

Tami pushed her sweat-dampened hair back from her brow, leaving a pattern of dark curlicues on her forehead. "Maybe Mom and Dad were right," she said. "Maybe it *was* just a sonic boom." She paused to pick burrs from her socks in a shaft of hot yellow sunlight piercing through the towering greenery.

"Didn't sound like it to me," Bud said, joining his sister as she sat down on a large tree stump. "But I'm not sure we're going to find any answers by tramping around out here anymore."

"Well, we've come this far," Tami said, wearily. "How about we just keep going and hike into town? We could buy a newspaper and see if anything was written up about the crash."

"Nope," Bud replied, dragging himself to his feet. "I'm sorry, but I'm done in. Besides, it's getting late. Let's head for home." He gazed around, trying to get his bearings. "Wanna take the trail through Eagle's Nest Gorge? It's faster."

"Yeah, whatever," Tami said with a yawn as she stooped beneath some low-hanging pine boughs and fell into stride with her brother.

A half-hour of trudging through the gorge straightened the curlicues of Tami's forehead into a row of dripping exclamation marks. "This isn't faster," she grumbled. "We should have gone back the same way we came."

"It *is* faster," Bud insisted, slightly offended.

"Look at the sun," Tami countered. "It's going to be dark by the time we—" She stopped herself, and stared straight ahead.

Bud saw what she was looking at, too. He took a tentative step forward, then gasped, "Wow, would you look at that!"

For several hundred yards or more all the trees up ahead had been smashed and shattered, making the gorge that Tami and Bud were walking in look like a forest of charred and broken toothpicks. At the end of the odd, smashed-up swatch of forest was a large, domed-shaped, silver craft, which had clearly made a crash landing. On impact it had dug a deep crater in the ground, where it now rested.

"Wow, it's a flying saucer," Bud muttered as he approached the craft, carefully picking his way over the gouged, splinter-covered ground.

"I can't believe it," Tami whispered, walking close behind her brother. "This is like something right out of a UFO book!"

Tami followed Bud as he jumped onto the dome, then one by one they lowered themselves into the deep cavity where the craft was half-buried. Huddled close together they peered inside a gaping hole in the metallic-looking side of the space vehicle. All looked dark and silent within.

"I'm going to have look inside," Bud declared. "Are you with me?"

"I guess," Tami said, her heart already pounding rapidly, her palms beginning to sweat.

Together they eased their way through the torn metal of the ship. Once inside, they waited for their eyes to adjust to the dim light, and slowly they realized they were not alone. Horrified, the two stared at a skeleton, slumped over a console, its bony hands still clutching the controls.

"It—it looks like a *human* skeleton!" Bud cried, his voice cracking with fear.

"Maybe it's some super-secret U.S. spacecraft that crashed a really long time ago," Tami suggested, stepping over debris that littered the floor.

"But the crash we heard was last night," Bud said. "This pilot has been dead a *long* time."

"Maybe he died in outer space years and years ago," Tami speculated. "And maybe this spaceship, or whatever it is, was on automatic pilot or something. Then, after years in space, it finally fell to earth."

"That's a possibility," Bud admitted. And then his eye caught sight of a smear of red on the console near where the skeleton's skull rested. He leaned over, dabbed at it with his finger, then took a whiff. "Yuck!" he gasped. "This is blood!"

"I don't get it," Tami said, leaning closer to examine the skeleton. "How could there be fresh blood on somebody who's been dead this long? It doesn't make any—"

But Tami's words caught in her throat. Inside the skeleton's fractured arm bone she saw what looked like greenish-yellow arteries snaking through a fleshy pink core.

"Uh, Bud," she whispered. "This skeleton isn't what it appears to be. I don't know what it is, but we'd better get—" Then she screamed as the skeleton's bony hand grabbed a tight hold on her wrist.

Do not be afraid, the skeleton said, as it squeezed the female human's arm. At the same time, it lifted its bleach-white skull from the console—bleach-white except for where bright red blood streamed down from a gash in its forehead. *My name is Legin, and I mean you no harm.*

Slowly, the male human was approaching, and judging by how the female was squirming, it was clear they did not understand him. Twin dots of green light moved in Legin's eye sockets as he looked at the humans. How could he tell the Earthlings not to be afraid? How could he communicate to them that he needed their help and nothing more?

I am Legin, he repeated, sending his thought communications as powerfully as he could. *I was the pilot of this craft, and I am hurt.* But clearly the humans were not picking up his telepathic messages.

Still holding onto the female human's arm, Legin saw that the male, though terrified, was now quite near and was about to attack him. *Stop!* Legin warned. *We do not need to harm one another!*

Though Legin knew the Earthling could not comprehend the language spoken on the space island Sonorious in the Cassiopian galaxy, he was pleased to see that somehow the hideous, flesh-covered being had apparently understood something. For it had stopped advancing, and was now just staring at him. Now if he could only get the male's female counterpart to stop struggling. If he could only make her stop emitting that painful sounding noise and simply calm down.

"It's alive!" Tami shrieked, trying to pull free of the hideous creature that apparently had flesh and blood *within* its bones. "Its body is inside its skeleton!"

Bud, who had begun creeping up on the creature now stood stark still, trying to decide the best way to free his sister. "Let her go!" he snarled. Then, feeling like he had no other means but force, Bud lunged at the skeleton and grabbed hold of its neck, squeezing with all his might.

A greenish glow that looked like a cross between panic and anger shown brightly in the skeleton's eyes. Instantly, it lost its grip on Tami and began to gag for breath as it clawed frantically at Bud's face.

"Ahhhhhh!" Bud cried. Grabbing his wounded cheek, he let go of the creature's bony neck, then slammed his fist into its pointy chin bone.

Tumbling backward, the skeleton struck its left temple on the edge of the console, and for a moment did not move.

"Run, Bud!" Tami yelled. "Run!"

Blood was dribbling from Bud's palm where it had made contact with the creature's sharp chin, and red slash marks lined his cheek. For a moment he stood panting, looking down at the bizarre creature at his feet. In so many ways it looked like, well, an inside-out human being.

"Come on, Bud!" Tami cried, pulling her brother by the front of his shirt. "Let's get out of here while we still can!"

As though coming out of a daze, Bud realized that his sister had already climbed out of the wrecked ship and was now hurrying away from the wounded craft. "I—I'm coming!" he called. Then with one last look at the strange skeletal being, he climbed through the wreckage and was on his sister's heels, racing toward their home.

Tami and Bud ran almost the entire way back to the cabin. Sweat-soaked, scraped, and terrified, they raced inside, looking as though they had just had a close encounter of the third kind—which they had.

"Mom! Dad!" they screamed, through the house, now dark and gloomy in the gathering twilight.

"What's wrong with you two?" their mother said, coming in through the back door. Wearing shorts and sandals, she put down the basket of vegetables she had been picking in the garden. "You look like you've seen a ghost."

Bud and Tami started talking at the same time. Their words came out in gasping gulps, overlapping and mixing together into a frenzied hodge-podge of jumbled incomplete sentences.

"Okay, okay," their mother said calmly. "Just try to slow down. You're not making any sense."

Just then Tami and Bud's father hurried in through the back door. His face was wrinkled up in a combination of confusion and disbelief since all he'd heard was a jumble of words that included "spacecraft," "living skeleton," and "crash." He told everyone to gather around the kitchen table and sit for moment. Then he looked at his two frightened children and asked, "Now, try to tell your mother and me exactly what happened—*slowly*."

Exhausted, still struggling to catch their breath, Tami and Bud each slumped into a chair. Then Tami began to explain as calmly as she could how they'd come upon the spacecraft.

Nursing his scraped hand, Bud picked up where Tami left off, telling his parents what they'd found inside the craft and how he had fought with the bizarre skeletal creature. Unable to keep still, he paced back and forth as he rambled through the story, repeatedly glancing out the window as though the creature would appear at any moment.

"We've got to get out of here," Tami concluded, rising to her feet as well. "That thing—whatever it was—is still alive!" She shuddered. "You should have seen it, Mom and Dad. It was a living skeleton! And it tried to kill us! I've never been so scared in my life!"

"A 'living skeleton,' huh?" Their dad looked from Tami to Bud, a trace of a smile on his face. "Boy, and I thought you two might be missing something by not having a television."

"Dad, we're not kidding!" Bud exclaimed.

"Yeah, Dad!" Tami cried. "We're not making this up! I mean it!"

"Sounds to me like you two went into town and read some of those stupid tabloids," their mother said, raising an eyebrow. "Am I right?"

"No!" the two kids exclaimed as one, both their voices laced with exasperation and terror.

Their dad winked at their mom. "Well, then I say let's go check out this space creature," he said, heading for the front door. "Who's with me?"

The others hurried after him, and no sooner had they all stepped out onto the porch, than the skeletal creature came walking toward them out of the dark woods, confirming Tami and Bud's fantastical story.

"Oh, my!" their mother exclaimed, pointing.

But their father could only stare, his mouth hanging open practically to the ground.

Upon seeing them, the skeleton appeared to walk faster, but when they all started scrambling around and screaming, it quickly turned and retreated into the shadows.

"It's the alien from the spaceship!" Bud yelled.

"How did it find us?" Tami whimpered. "What does it want?"

"Stay calm, everybody!" their dad exclaimed, suddenly finding his voice. "Just run to the car—fast!"

"I'll get the keys!" their mom yelled, already darting into the house. She returned moments later and the four piled into the station wagon.

"Come on, come on!" groaned their dad, trying to coax to life an engine that only got started once or twice a month. He pumped the accelerator furiously, but the ignition refused to turn over. Finally, there was a rattling sound, the starter growled, and suddenly the engine roared to life. A moment later the station wagon was squealing away into the night.

In the back seat, Tami and Bud were staring silently out the windows of the car, while in the front their parents kept saying things like "We're all right," and "There's no way it can catch us now."

But their encouraging words were suddenly cut off when both kids let out cries of terror.

"There it is!" Bud screamed, pointing to the two green dots of light emerging from the black forest. "I can see its eyes!"

"How can it run so fast?" Tami cried, as the skeleton came stumbling toward them, its stark-white arms outstretched.

"Hang on!" their dad yelled. "I think I can lose it!"

The rear wheels screeching, the station wagon kicked up clumps of sod as it tore through a grassy stretch and skittered onto a dirt road, leaving a huge cloud of dust in its wake.

"You did it, Dad!" Bud yelled, his eyes glued to the rear window. "I don't see it anymore!"

"I don't either!" Tami cried happily.

The car bucked and jolted down the rutted road. It fishtailed through a sharp turn, then there was a heart-stopping thud as they sideswiped a tree.

"Please, slow down, honey!" their mother yelled. "I think you've lost it!"

But her warning was too late, the car had already bounced off the tree and was now careening down an embankment. Glass shattered and metal came apart with loud, banging crunches as the station wagon tumbled end over end down the cliff, finally crumpling to a stop in a jagged crevasse.

For a moment all was still, save a few stones bounding down from where the car was wedged into the deep cleft of stone and hard-packed soil. Then a solitary hubcap clattered down the mountainside. It was bouncing away into the night when the ruptured gas tank of the McNeil's station wagon suddenly exploded with a socking *whoomf*, engulfing what was left of the car in a huge, rolling ball of flame.

Legin found the twisted wreckage the next day. Somberly he carried each of the bodies back to the small log cabin. There he tended to them, amazed to find that under their flesh were bones just like his.

Why were they afraid of me? he kept wondering as he worked to breathe life into their bodies. *It was I who should have been afraid of them.* He shook his head, lost in confusion. *What an odd world these humans live in,* he decided. *And now it is my world.*

The rains came early and especially hard that year. The pines sagged beneath the downpour, rivers swelled, mud flowed. As it stormed, wedges of claylike soil dropped onto the wreckage of the station wagon where it was crammed nose-down in the crevasse. Soon, chunks of rock collapsed onto it and the earth around it—which had turned into a thick, liquidy mess—slowly covered up the car, and eventually swallowed it whole.

Not too far away, in a desolate stretch of forest, mud filled a peculiar cavity in the earth, burying a silver, domed craft that no human—other than a teenage brother and sister—had ever laid eyes on. During a lull between the heavy rains, Legin visited this spot. In silence, feeling desolate and empty, he gazed at the mucky patch below which his ship lay buried. He now knew he would never return to Sonorious. Never again would he see his family and friends. Heartsick and sad, he made his way back through the forest.

As usual, once back in the cabin, he felt better. It was almost as though he were with his own kind, for he had scraped the burned flesh from their bones and scrubbed and cleaned the bodies. Now four skeletons sat with him in the room. The two smaller ones—a male and female, sat on the couch. The larger female and male each sat in chairs. Often Legin sat with them, holding their hands and talking to them. Though they never answered back, they allowed him to pretend he was back home. They made him feel less lonely. After all, they looked just like him now, so normal sitting there, so natural, so lifelike.

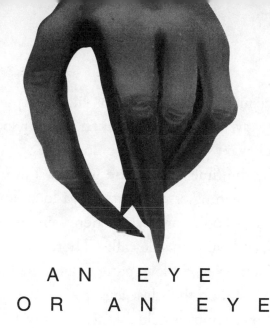

AN EYE
FOR AN EYE

bigail died yesterday morning. And Ovid this afternoon. As for me, I don't even have the strength to drag out the bodies. It's just me in here, in this horrid-smelling room. Mold on the walls, trash all over, and dusty sunlight filtering in through the musty drapes—that's what it's like in this terrible place.

Though it hurts a lot, I force myself to my feet and off of this grimy sofa bed. Slowly—like an old man—I shuffle across the room. I'm only fourteen, but I feel like I'm over a hundred. I stop in the middle of the room and turn and see myself in the mirror above the table. I'm so sick and so wretched-looking I hardly recognize myself anymore. I look like a corpse, like I'm dead already, with my eyes sunken in their sockets and my skin a waxy yellow-white color.

By the time I reach the window I'm totally out of breath. Leaning on the dirty sill, I look down at the street. Dead bodies are everywhere—in the stores, in the cars, and lying on sidewalks. There aren't even any animals left, except a few mangy, sickly-looking rats—and they're all on their last legs, too.

I break into a cold sweat, and my head aches. Just walking across the room—a simple thing like that—is too much for me.

Suddenly I'm dizzy, but I manage to get to a chair and sit down. It's so quiet, so deathly quiet. The only sound is the ticking of the clock on the bookcase near where Ovid and Abigail lie. If only they weren't dead I'd have someone to talk to, something to listen to besides that miserable ticking clock.

But I'm pretty sure I'm the only person left. Maybe there are a few more like me—the living dead, that is—but what could they do for me? What could I do for them?

Nothing.

All I can do is sit here, listening to the silence, unable to stop my mind from looping back around and around to the way it started … back to that horrible day at the zoo.

It seems like it was centuries ago. But it wasn't. In fact, it was exactly one month ago that all this misery started—August 8, 2103. It was my birthday. And my dad told me that I could go anywhere or do anything I wanted. "It's *your* day, Falkner," he'd said. "We'll do whatever *you* want, pal!"

I remember how all kinds of possibilities popped into my head. I could have taken the underwater train to Europe for the day. I could have whisked through the two thousand-mile drainpipe ride or ridden the four-hour roller coaster at 250 Flags Over the Planet. I could have even gone down the thermal-tube to see the inside of the earth.

But my sister Kezzy kept after me about going to the brand-new Alien Zoo that had opened in Atlanta last year. Not only was it supposed to be the best in the world with just about all the weirdest aliens ever found, now they were advertising a brand-new "capture"—an Icarian. "Plucked fresh from the jungles of Icaria, the least explored of the four planets in Canis Minor!" the ad in the paper had blared. "Come see the amazing, the bizarre Icarian!"

Yup, it was the chance to see this freaky new alien that finally made me decide on going to the zoo for my birthday. It was a bad decision.

Nevertheless, we went. We—Kezzy, my parents, and I—boarded the air-train which took us from New

Jersey to Atlanta in the usual ten minutes. Then, after a four-second transport ride, we were walking through the great iron gates of the Alien Zoo.

The place was absolutely gigantic, with acres and acres of cages and open-air exhibits, the kind where the animals are allowed to wander free. Food stands, games, rides—there were tons of those, too—and they even had an old-fashioned train, a rebuilt one from way back in the 20th century, to take you wherever you wanted to go.

The first alien animals we saw were the monkey-tails, which look just like the tails of monkeys, coiled and hanging from trees, only there's no monkey on the other end. And roaming all around in the enclosure with them were Terra cervidae, commonly known as sander deer, because they're like regular deer except their hides look and supposedly feel like sandpaper. Best of all were the pedepods, which are found mostly in Ursa Major. Pedepods are just legs that walk around in cages. The funny thing about them is that they don't have any eyes or a sense of direction, and they're always tripping and falling over each other. Everybody was hysterical over them. And me, they just about cracked me up. I think I could have stayed there watching the pedepods all day.

Next we went to the Ornithological Exhibit and saw millions of different kinds of strange birds. But it got sort of boring after a while, and Kezzy was getting impatient. She wanted to go to the Herpetological House, but Mom refused, saying they had cannibal snakes in there. Now these guys are super gross! By their name, you'd think they'd eat each other, but they don't. Instead, when a cannibal snake gets hungry enough, it loops around and, starting at the tail, it devours itself!

Anyway, not even Kezzy's obnoxious pleading would change Mom's mind, and since Dad sided with her, we ended up going to the Aquatic Exhibit. Kezzy was pouty and grumpy for a while. But she snapped out of it a few minutes after we got on the moving sidewalk, which took us past miles and miles of plasti-tanks filled with stone sharks, intestine fish, tongue worms, bunny-heads, clacker eels, and a thousand other kinds of undersea creatures from all over the galaxy.

After lunch, we piled onto the air-rail and took it to the other side of the zoo. By then it was afternoon, and the place was really beginning to fill up. There must have been a zillion people in that zoo, and it seemed like most of them were in the New Species Zone. It was totally jam-packed—especially around the Icarian's cage. We squeezed through the crowd and got to the front. And then I saw it.

Well, I have to tell you, the thing scared the heck out of me! I mean, I've seen uglier aliens, but this creature really made my skin crawl. In a way, it was plain-looking—sort of like a faceless, featureless boy. It had no color, and it wasn't really doing anything except standing there behind the bars, motionless. It had only been in captivity for a couple of days, and you could see it was real unhappy—and mad enough to kill.

Anyway, like I said, the Icarian had no facial features, except sometimes I could see a huge, single, ectoplasmic eye appear beneath the semi-transparent skin of its face. It was at that moment that I knew the creature was watching us Earthlings who'd come to watch it. The eye was easy to see once it appeared, but then it would sort of recede until the face was totally blank again.

"The Icarian is one of the hardest aliens in the universe to capture," a young woman in a tan uniform was telling the crowd. She gestured toward the Icarian's cage with her tiny solar microphone. "Early trappers claimed that the Icarians have an uncanny ability to elude capture. They suspected that the creatures have an extremely high IQ, and a chameleonic ability—that is, an ability to somehow change and blend with things in their environment. And if that isn't enough, these extraordinary aliens are said to have a natural, built-in sonar system."

"What does 'sonar' mean?" asked a little boy in the audience.

"Sonar," the guide explained with a smile, "is the transmission of high-frequency sound waves. It is used to locate things—sometimes at great distances."

"And this Icarian can do that?" another little boy wanted to know.

"At this point we're not exactly sure what the Icarian is capable of doing," the spokeswoman answered. "Actually, we know very little about Icarians. In fact, the one we have here is the very first ever captured, and we haven't yet run any tests on it. It is, however, as far as we can determine, a very young specimen—and *that* perhaps may be the reason we were able to catch it."

"What do you mean?" a man asked.

"Perhaps it wasn't fully aware of its powers at the time it was captured." The woman smiled. "So, perhaps *it,* as well as *we,* still have a lot to learn about what Icarians can do."

As the woman kept talking, I was getting kind of jittery. For some reason, the Icarian had singled me out of the crowd and was staring at me. Actually, it didn't feel like it was just staring at me. It felt like the odd creature was looking right *through* to my soul.

It was very unsettling and I was relieved when we moved on to the next exhibit. But no matter how hard I tried, I couldn't seem to get the Icarian out of my mind. I wanted to go back to see it. No, I was *compelled* to go back to see it.

But my folks weren't very interested and neither was Kezzy. She said she would only go with me if I got her a treat. So, after I bought us each giant Icebar Slurpcicles—chocolate for me and strawberry for her— we agreed on a place to meet up with our parents later, and the two of us went back to see what the Icarian was was doing now.

As we stood there in front of its cage, slurping away, the Icarian's eye emerged, and I could swear the thing recognized me.

"Who do you think you're staring at, ugly?" I yelled self-consciously, laughing on the outside, but cringing on the inside.

But the Icarian didn't even flinch … or stop staring. It just kept looking right at me—no, not at me, *into* me—its one weird eye not blinking even once.

"Wow," Kezzy said with a shudder. "It looks like it hates you."

"Who cares?" I sneered. "I'm not the one in the cage—*it* is. Aren't you, you ugly slab of meat?" I called to the Icarian, taunting it for all I was worth.

Its eye was still on me.

"Oh, so you want to have a staring contest, do you?" I asked like a big shot. "Well, I got the odds on my side. Two against one! My two eyes against your one eye."

"Go for it!" Kezzy exclaimed, cheering me on and giggling with excitement.

I made a face and then I locked eyes with the Icarian, trying not to blink, trying not to be afraid. But I *was* afraid. And I couldn't help myself … I blinked.

"Guess you lost," Kezzy said with a shrug. "Come on, let's go meet Mom and Dad."

"Oh, yeah?" I snarled. Angry, I scooped up some of my chocolate Slurpcicle and flung it at the Icarian. That's when it moved for the first time. Well, actually it didn't just move, it lunged at me, slamming into the bars of its cage.

Startled, I jumped back and I threw my whole Slurpcicle at it—right at that miserable eye which now, for the first time, blinked.

"Ha! *You* lose!" I yelled, bending over with laughter when I saw the gooey Slurpcicle dripping down the Icarian's face.

Well, *that* really set it off! Its eye went wide with rage and it started rattling the bars like it had gone crazy, like it would do anything to get out of that cage and tear me to shreds.

"Let's get out of here!" yelped Kezzy.

"I'm not scared of old Cyclops in there!" I said, but still I backed away with her. Then we ran, laughing nervously all the way to the folder munk cage, where we were supposed to meet our parents.

As soon as we saw them, Kezzy and I launched into a jabbering frenzy, telling our parents what had happened with the Icarian. I, naturally, acted real cool like I wasn't bothered by the creature at all. But after a while, I realized that our parents didn't seem to be paying much attention, anyway, they were busy gawking at the folder munks. Even I got caught up in watching the funny little beasts.

Found on several of the planets and asteroids in the Orestrian Galaxy, folder munks keep their young in little pouches on their heads. They sort of look like chipmunks with furry wings, and when they get scared, they fold up behind their wings and hide. Anyway, we were standing there looking at the cute little guys when we heard a commotion near the New Species Zone. Then someone screamed and a man ran by yelling, "The Icarian escaped, and it got a kid!"

About that time just about everybody started running toward the Icarian exhibit—including me and my family. When we got there, everyone was pretty much in a state of panic or disbelief.

"Doesn't make any sense," a groundskeeper was saying to a snake-a-loons vendor who had joined the crowd gathered in front of the Icarian's cage. "Why did it put the kid in there?"

Tons of people were all around the cage now, almost completely blocking my view. But by standing on my tiptoes I caught a glimpse of some guy about my age yelling to be let out. Little by little, my family and

I edged forward. And then my mouth dropped open in disbelief. I mean, I thought I'd lose my mind at what I saw. The kid in the cage was ... *me*!

My parents and Kezzy were bonking out, too, looking back and forth from me to the guy in the cage. Me, I was frozen in terror. Then I spotted a zookeeper who was as frantic as everyone else. He was searching for the right code-key to the cage, sweat dripping down from his temples. In a zombielike daze I watched him. It wasn't until he found the right code-key and was about to unlock the swingdoor that I came back to life.

"Don't let him out!" I screeched, terrified. "Something's wrong!"

But there was so much noise and confusion that nobody seemed to hear. And already, the boy—the boy who looked exactly like me—was out of the cage. He jumped to the ground right in front of me, looked me right in the eye ... and flashed me a chilling smile. Then he just walked away.

Shaken to the bone, my mind reeling, I knew what had happened, and what the Icarian had done. It had turned itself into a copy of me, and now it looked like just any ordinary kid heading for the exit.

"Stop that boy!" I yelled. "He's the Icarian and he's getting away!"

A woman in a green jumpsuit wearing a badge was running toward the scene with a bunch of security people right on her heels. She looked like somebody important, like maybe the zoo's director. Whoever she was, she was suddenly asking me a hundred questions. I tried to explain as best I could what had happened and that the Icarian was getting away. I ran and pointed to where I had last seen the creature disguised as my twin. But the boy—the Icarian—had been swallowed up in the crowd.

I was really shaken up by the time we got home. And the next day I didn't go to school. Feeling totally freaked out, I stayed indoors all day long, too scared to go anywhere.

Lots of people came to visit me, including my Aunt Adelle, who's real cool and knows how to talk to kids. She came from all the way across town to sit with me for a while and try to make me feel better.

"It wasn't your fault," she told me, giving me a warm hug. "That Icarian probably hated everybody who was looking at it, and would have escaped whether you'd made fun of it or not."

While we were talking, the stereophone beeped. It was my dad, calling from work, and he sounded real upset. In fact, by the way his voice was shaking, I think he'd been crying. "Sit down," he told me. "I hate to have to tell you this but—"

"But what?" I asked, suddenly anxious. "What's wrong, Dad?"

"The police just called. Your Aunt Adelle was found murdered in her house this morning and—"

I looked up in horror at the person I thought was my Aunt Adelle. Then I screamed, suddenly realizing who—or rather, *what*—she really was.

"Why are you doing this?" I screamed at the monster who was in the shape of my aunt.

Laughing, the Icarian walked toward me, still an exact twin of my aunt. And since I was pretty much frozen in terror, all I could do was just stare at her as she brought her face right up next to mine.

"What are you staring at, ugly?" she asked, an evil grin on her face. And then she let out the most horrible laugh I'd ever heard, turned, and walked out the door.

Of course, the story about the Icarian's escape was in just about every newspaper and magazine ever printed, and I was interviewed by every media hound around. I told them all that I knew about the Icarian, and in the days that followed there were all sorts of bizarre stories about me, and even more stories about the Icarian circulating around the world. For example, there was an article about a man in Canada who claimed to have awakened one morning to find *himself* sitting in a chair next to his bed. Then there was another story about an ophthalmologist who lost his mind when he found himself staring into his *own* eyes.

And maybe grossest of all the weird stories was the one about the actress who disappeared—then reappeared three days later ... carrying her own dead body.

All the stories were pretty horrible and super freaky. But they were nothing compared to what was to come. That's when the *real* horror began.

It started with an emergency alert from the director of SWR—Satellite War Reconnaissance. He reported that the hostile Indo-European Republic, a federation of countries in South Europe, was preparing for a preemptive strike on the United States and its Mid-Asian allies. According to the director, the Indo-European Republic was fueling ancient but still lethal ICBMs—Intercontinental Ballistic Missiles—and it was prepared to launch a nuclear strike on the United States in five minutes.

At first the President, as I understand it, was skeptical. But then he had a sudden change of heart—*very* sudden.

The order came from the Oval Office and our own nuclear and neutron missiles were launched—by the thousands. None of the countries had enough time to retaliate. Europe, Asia, South America, and Africa—they were all reduced to ashes in less than twenty minutes.

And then the United States was hit, not by nuclear or neutron weapons, but by provender bombs, the most sickening weapon of war ever devised. They don't damage buildings, bridges, or structures of any kind. No, these horrible destroyers release a chemical called Enzymatic T-22 that attacks the internal organs of living creatures—the digestive organs in particular. It's disgusting how this man-made enzyme works. You see, it doesn't kill quickly. No, it causes the body to slowly digest itself!

At first we didn't know where the provenders were coming from. All other countries, as far as we knew, had been destroyed. Not until later, after it was pretty much all over, did it become known that the order to launch these terrible missiles—and target them on the U. S.—had come from the Capitol ... directly from the President himself.

For a while there was live videoramic coverage of provenders exploding like huge shotgun blasts from one end of the U. S. to the other. Then, as people began dying in droves and everything was sheer chaos, the broadcasts ceased. New Jersey, where I'm from, was the last place hit, and I realized that's the way the Icarian wanted it. It wanted me to see the horror. It wanted me to see my family, my friends, and everybody else being carted off to hospitals, dying by the score, or driven nearly insane with fear and pain.

Now don't get me wrong. The Icarian hated everybody—*all* people—for capturing it. But it was *me* it hated most. And to that end, it had chosen *me* to be the last to die. Yes, the Icarian had decided that I was its nemesis, and for that I was to see the power of what it could do and all the suffering that it could cause.

I'm sure by now you've figured out who the man—or should I say monster—in the Oval Office was. And I'm sure you could guess at least some of the other steps the Icarian took—careful and intelligent steps—to get back at me and my kind. But what exactly became of the Icarian after he'd pretty much destroyed the world, I don't know. My guess is that the creature probably died, not even caring if it killed itself in the process of getting its revenge on humankind.

Anyway it doesn't matter whether the Icarian is dead or alive. It won.

As for me, I sleep a lot, or at least I try to. You see, I'm kind of jumpy these days and the slightest sound wakes me up. Mostly, it's dead quiet, though, and the only sounds are the ones in my head—the *memory* of sounds, of life going on as it used to.

In my mind I hear planes overhead, cars passing by, and people. I hear them walking down the sidewalk, and having normal conversations. Sometimes I hear—

Wait a minute! What I'm hearing this very instant is *not* the memory of footsteps. No, what I'm hearing at this very moment are *real* footsteps ... and they're coming up the stairs.

Shaking violently, I sit up, and my heart leaps into my throat when I hear a little knock on the door. Then the door screeches open, and Kezzy peeks in!

"You're alive!" I yell happily.

She walks across the room toward me.

"Kezzy?"

She smiles at me and all I can do is stare at her, my face blank with confusion.

Still smiling, she sits down next to me, and then her smile disappears. "Who do you think you're staring at, ugly?" she asks, then breaks into the most horrible laugh I've ever heard.